Inside In

Poems

Linda Chown

**Inside In
Copyright © 2015 Linda Chown**

ALL RIGHTS RESERVED. This book contains material protected under International and Federal Copyright Laws and Treaties. Any unauthorized reprint or use of this material is prohibited. No part of this book may be reproduced or transmitted in any form or by any means, electronic or mechanical, including photocopying, recording, or by any information storage and retrieval system without express written permission from the author / publisher.

Author Contact: LindaChown@hotmail.com

ISBN: 978-1-940164-28-1

Cover thanks to Amy Cole, Director of Design, at JPL Design Solutions. She shaped my preliminary images into a beautiful cover which features on the back, Vincent van Gogh, "Piles of French Novels and Roses in a Glass" ("Romans Parisiens"), c. 1887. The front cover is an irresistible street in Cádiz, Spain.

Printed in the United States of America

For Buck

> It is not to touch
> Patterns to the world
> But to pattern touching
> Francis Hosman

CONTENTS

I. PLACE

Passing Salt Flats in San Fernando, Spain 3
A Small Geography of Eternity 4
Good Friday Night in Madrid 5
Cosmological T-Group with Flowers 7
A Psalm for Cádiz 8
Anti-Lyric 10
A New Look at Conil Through Your Eyes 11
Hotel Blues in Brindisi 12
In Winter, When the Tourists Are Gone 13
Monday Metaphysics 15
More Than the Dying and the Wars and Our Words About Them 17
Semana Santa: Holy Week in Spain 18
Two Years in Europe Poem 20
Nebbish on Holiday 21
Words and Bees at the SF Marina 22
When the Blue Light Went Off 24
Brought Up To Music 26
Making It So Easy To See 27
Birthday in Moscow 28
Homage to a Jamaican Stone-Carver 29
Sit-In: Sheraton Palace I: April 1964 30
When on a Long Night 32
2012: Summer Without Rain 33
How Where We Were Was 34
Green Fantasies: After Lewis Carroll 35

II. PEOPLE

Death at 52 39
After the Heart Attack 40
Uncle Sasha 41
Echoes of Exotic 43
For My English Student 44
Part Payment 45

v

Don't Ask 47
On the Other Side of Language.. 49
The Young Widow 51
The Little Lamb 52
Strange Man.. 54
To the Second Doorman 55
Abortion 56
School Days... 57
Standing Out in the Straight 58
Missing 59
Meeting... 63
Roots Taking Hold.. 65
Wood Sight... 66

III. KNOWINGS

Out West When Clouds Rolled Over 71
Some Times Writing 72
Sometimes We Can't Keep Up.. 73
To Say Thinking 74
Where We Are In 75
Writing To... 76
On Reading Old Poems 77
Shore-Lines in the Sand 78
Writing in Place 79
When The Sun Is 81
There Was Never Enough Home 83
And There They Were 84
Flower Juice 86
Politics is What
People Do 87
To Be or To Be 89
Too Many Moons.. 90
About the Lion 91
And He Thought He Said 92
A Kind of a Love Poem... 93
To an Unknown Painter 94
The Gift.. 95

Red Around the Center 96
Out of the Wind 97
How To Say What 98

These poems were written during many times, places, ideas, and intensities, I often remember Franz Kafka, his idea of "the infinite life" as a way of always living in life. In a similar spirit, Spanish novelist Carmen Martín Gaite once told me, "Hay que habitar la soledad."

Place

the intimacy of the physical world
Galway Kinnell

Passing Salt Flats in San Fernando, Spain

Strange to be reminded of Japanese
men, of watercolor films tidy
as a plane's eye's view:
squares, vaguely green and brown
patches and wiry men
padding, barefooted in loose pants
and wide-brimmed hats
over the salt field's flats.
They are hoeing salt from the land's pockets
here on the edge of Europe
which the full tide has filled.

Regal this, like a coronation
in its form and I remember more
of the Japanese woman
drawing water, of the monk's
purposefully shaved head and towns
of dark wood and mats of straw,
towns whose paper walls
open into light
like a quiet maze of rivers.

But here, now, the bus races
like a fool through history
past the mud flats and whitewashed shacks, bouncing and
heaving on the narrow road,
its glass eyes glittering
greedy to arrive
while just outside
the sun is high
and the world suddenly old and silent.
A chorus of men digging their toes
into earth and the salt seems to quiver
in the wind with all the beauty at can be on the road of San Fernando.

Conil de la Frontera

A Small Geography of Eternity

I.
At the edge of the forest
a beam of sunlight
strikes the field of redwoods.
Morning. The air clear,
smelling of pine needles
and oil. Camp fires burning.
I step over charred, heavy logs,
look into empty cabins,
and stare at their clean wood rooms.
No pictures hang on these walls.
The green wreath on that door
has gone limp forever.
A gunning of an engine.
The air still clear.
II.
The silence of the forest
surrounds me,
invisible,
the shape of a poem.
III.
More wood chips
settle into
the floor of this forest
than I ever can pick.
V.
On the way home to San Francisco
I learn to take curves at 60 miles an hour.
I am near death
and what is eternity but
everything that is and
everything that is not around
me.

Stinson Beach

Good Friday Night in Madrid

I stood on the corner of a wide boulevard
where green taxis pulled at
the slow moving crowds.
The whole world turned black
on Good Friday night
and the resurrection
just around the corner,
the people all ready,
the women veiled to death,
the men dressed up little boys,
the air so quiet you couldn't hear
the bells ringing,
the old gray church doors flung open,
and all round the block
a sober black procession.

Down in the subway alleys,
people scurried along the platforms,
running for trains.
From all directions they came
in their best black clothes.
Moving with them, I
pushed into a second class car
between four short men,
stood with them
in the smoke and wet air.
Our street clothes wrinkled.
The whole car creaked.
The men pressed their slim thighs
against me steady as drills.
They held tight to the straps,
pressing.
The lights flickered,
The overhead fan squeaked.

There was no way out.
My hand reached
out for the arm straps.
I felt a steady pushing
and the silence of people
clinging together
like bats taking off in the dark.

Cosmological T-Group with Flowers

I.
Red flowers
by the sea coast
blooming in cold fog

dark weeds bending
in the wind the
ocean dancing the steep
cliffs the violet-blue weeds
glowing the country sprawling
the road curves
the coast—
these flowers
their showing

II.
This way earth
breeds itself in the swell
and root of salt.
Nourished by the damp air,
things grow
simply
a plan for us
after all
lies in the bright
dance of flowers
loose along the sea.

Stinson Beach

A Psalm for Cádiz

Death is in your peeling walls
Cádiz, in those skies that carry clouds
so lightly, in the cups of wine
and throat-wrenched songs in bars,
in the sinuous turnings of your dirty
streets. Death in the boats
that bring our pretty fish.
Death in the wind that swallows
our pretty words.
Death in the rats in our garbage

And you seem to take more of women.
You seem to eat their hearts out,
the biggest of them who come
to love you and your off beat ways
I hate the webs you sew:
One buried in the non-believer's graves,
nervous, wild-eyed woman, no friend
of mine, whose tiny taut bones
are rotting, nurtured by a
deaf Spanish gardener in the shade
of his days.
One a woman of spirit, of art,
my godmother by blood, a friend
at the end, who lost all her breathing
and her heart to lie adrift
in the dark she hated.
One a woman for beauty and grace
who's losing her energy and spirit
in this crumbling place.

Inevitable deaths and sickening, I
know, but there's something in your ways,
in those long 3000 years of fires
and plague and pillage that haunt,
that live in your unearthly winds

like buzzards fly, keeping even the tourists
away. Your walls must be made of bones
for all the buried here.
The fishes rich with English blood
still. The tide replete with long
lost wishes. So, when the wind sings
like it does today under the doors
I'm brought, premature, to dungeons
and morgues, to the sucklings of worms
and unperceived crumblings of earth.

I've come to despise your pride in the sea
rushing as it does over buried walls
and faces of an older Cádiz I'll never see.
I fear to never leave here,
to be taken by surprise
and blent into the background
with the wild sea birds singing
but a token song for me.

Death is in your walls, Cádiz,
in the faces of a people
who know the ocean always
closes around the empty places.

Anti-Lyric

All day I've wanted to press my skin
my breasts my hands against a memory.
I desinhabit these rooms.
I look backward constantly.
It's not love of man
that makes this marrow smell,
these words flag breathlessly.
It's all those faces in an American summer,
all those semi-sweet lives just beyond reach.

My god, freeways look beautiful from here
and that's bad.
Must be the pain of exile got me
for tonight I would exchange all your crises
for this heartless tranquility
and this end of the world feeling.
I want to sit in your rooms
well barricaded against thiefs
and let all your stories and theories
and griefs rush over me
in a great familiar tide
tonight as I sit on the edge
of a continent, feeling something's
wrong, that tomorrow's said
too many times over,
while this aging Spanish sea feathers
a disconsolate impersonal song
and everything exactly exactly
as it seems to be.

Cádiz

A New Look at Conil Through Your Eyes

> to Mignonne and Abe

Sometimes, in this fishing village
of white houses and black shadow
miles off the main road
I have wondered where the old questions went—
of what is what and why
and how they sank with this orange sun
into a glittering sea
and in their place—shadows
broke on the walls
and the day's long routine
stuck in blue light
like dead fish wedged
tight in wicker baskets.

The day you came we walked and talked,
played for hours in the sand.
You took the place and said to me:
this town is ghosted with shade
and shapes. It echoes sight
and sound. It breathes ocean smells
and flowers. It takes the old reasoning mind
and cry and burns it fine and clean as baby skin.
It says see, live again,
poetry is possible
let the questions be
part of the poem,
part of the church bell's ring in midday
part of the rhythm that makes
today tomorrow
part of the old richness.

Hotel Blues in Brindisi

Sad fish mouth in the mirror
What makes you stick out in space
like a star fixed and drifting?
I lock it up with the eyes.
swimming nowhere really
in a baggy no-horse hotel
where Beckett might even be
for it's night here always
and nothing is seen to be.

Waiting is a bone, unfed.
And time is the coffee toy
with the baby's screams.
Space the shitty floors
and the telephone rings.
Heart is what happened once.
Thought is a threat
and I the accompaniment
of some loose-knitted thread.

White bones and baby shit.
Pimps home, a-jingling.

Oh, sad fish mouth,
in a dark hotel room
you are so gullible
and wrinkled pink
you are.

Hold on tight again
and twinkle.

In Winter, When the Tourists Are Gone

How far from the common ideas of Spain,
a land of wine and castles and castanets
are the fading streets of any secondary town
and its drudgery of iron-barred windows.
its banks and bars and babies
where scrawny dogs limp in the dirt for food.
It's tiny dim-lit neighborhood stores
where crowds of gigantic women rub behinds.
and dead cats rot untouched in the alleys.
It's broken glass and garbage and uniforms
of soldiers, children and the roundelay
of ladies dragging their carts to market every day.

It's trudge and drudge and doubtful hopes.
Blind lottery vendors sell tickets in the dark,
buttons missing on a gray stained coat.
It's two jobs daily and a quart of beer.
The sun's no object. It's an unforgetting witness
here to these ghost town streets
where when the tourists are gone in winter
the buildings look like barracks
and the things of this world keep running
into one another in a dissonant way
as though the loss of them and their glitter
made less of hope. It's back to beans
again and sweaters and cold in the bones.
It's back to the houses, those empty shells
are overcrowded, overheated rooms of stone.

Subject now to the skies whimsy
the heart, that famous southern fire, hibernates
and sheds the exotic skins of summer
in this most Arabic part of Spain
where it will rain and rain
washing the streets clean of its leavings
and the envy tourists have sown

in order to take pride in Christmas
and the people can make the un-equivocating streets
completely though bitterly again
their own.

Monday Metaphysics

> Things entirely themselves arriving in the deep
> Double shadows of the grass and passersby.
> Kathy Fagan

It is the most open time.
Ringing church bells at no special hours.
And newspaper headlines flit
tiny scores of music
in a cooler autumn air.

I do not know what calls me.
These streets are old and bare
and rocky steep. Days repeat
like watersheds in blue fog.

Am I waiting
for something other
than that dry broom outside
scraping dust into Sunday air
or the harsh garble
of yapping talk in the street?

Like a cat cleaning under its tail
in the corner of a large barn
I keep the movements going
through outdoor markets
with plumpened women
who stake their finds with hardened eyes
and lift those heavy baskets
beyond their wildest girlhood dreams.

Like the cat keeping at it
I stick my arms through the harness
and lift ten pounds of food
wedged tight into three bulky old bags.
It's just 10:30 but all there is

in these brown Granada streets
with the crisp air of centuries past
is the weight of this present
and tedious doing socked into my side
every step upward the hill.

More Than the Dying and the Wars and Our Words About Them

To sit here on this roof
with the Sierra Nevada mountains
in my mouth
and the Alhambra's blossoming
gardens up my nose
and the tiled brown roofs
sloping and arching below me—
to sit here and be here
smoking, alive, sizzling a bit
in the sun.

Newspapers say nothing about this.
They want to make us
afraid.
They say people are dying
and the world's all   up.

I know I will go
behind the mountain
falling like a great snow-
covered cloud drifting,
and people are dying,
swollen up with need,
inching their way
through their way
like baby ants buried
under gray sand.

Take the papers away
and spread the world out
on the table.
Let's eat it for breakfast
if we can.

Semana Santa: Holy Week in Spain

Widows smooth their long shawls at dusk,
closing lottery sales for the day.
Corners swell up.
The pursed smile of evening
touches wide, milling streets.
Waiting cabbies seduce their fares.
At 6 pm the world comes alive,
stores open their grates,
mink and oranges
beckon like magnets.
People promenade,
their broad faces echoing
on the gardened streets.
Hand in hand they march
in pressed dark suits
away from children
in cave houses.
The crowded subway rides
blackened figures, seared in heat
who sway divided and quieted
in the sad thrust of angry tired flesh.

In the Plaza de Roma
American soldiers fire
their large bodies
down Spanish streets.
When night hits dusk
he leads his women
towards the dance halls,
those oceans of protocol
where fulsome women
with heavy painted faces
stalk around,
money running down their thighs.
Downtown, cafes center square wooden rooms
for business men beginning their work.

Dusk is heavy with scent,
redolent with motion.
Groomed women, sternly escorted,
packs of men, immaculate in black,
plunder the slow streets,
clapping their hands.

From a hidden balcony a woman coughs,
takes a long colored sheet banner and
hangs it from her window, displaying
for Franco, for God, for Spain.
Her doorbell sounds.
She greets two Americans,
she couldn't possibly ever hear.
Coughing lightly into her clothes,
she puts them in a double room,
opens the window, smoothes the ironed sheet
and disappears.

Madrid's nightly promenades
melt into one larger procession.
Flags wave, banners wave down.
The streets, dotted with color,
And the highest dignitaries:
holy men form in klans,
wearing color sheets.
They cover their faces with pointed slits.
Invisible politicians stride in gray suits.
Police flank the cluttered square.

From a balcony one stifled cough
echoes into the peopled night.
A woman hastens to the plaza,
thistles drooping from her head.
In her right hand a chain
drags a heavy clanging ball.
She moves slowly into the square.

Easter has come to Spain.

Two Years in Europe Poem

I on the bed, shutters half-closed,
staring into the vacant holes
of an apartment half–done
the autumn sun casts a tinted yellow,
a mellow hue I look through
to the two years of living here
and all the many suns I drew,
of wind and rain and random thiefs,
of gray hair coming and the griefs,
of full skies and autumn feasts;
no future it seems,
no surprises yet to come.

I lie ensconced in the heavy
cradle of the present.
These partial rhymes come like months
of light do, like I do,
passing through, passing through
the half-remembered glory
of wind-sounds and lip sounds
and the sun always off somewhere
writing her great orange story
in the lines of the sky
while I lie, trying to conjure something
solid out of my being
here so long.

Cádiz

Nebbish on Holiday

At eight I went to a fair
and dragged my mother to the roller coaster
there. It was rusty and high, delightfully old.
I was young and fresh and stupidly bold.
The attendant looked like Audie Murphy.
He said, *Look y'all, strap in like so, you see*
His big blue eyes cast a social glance on me.
I leaped to my seat and he fled to his hut.
There was a screech of brakes
and a terrible thud.

Audie came running with his cheeks
all red. *What are you doing?* he said.
Have you lost your head?
I was sitting pretty on the part for your feet.
There up above me was the empty seat
and the ground down below.
Mother came flying in through the wire gate,
lines of worry all over her face.
She whisked me away to a shady grove
where over the camp stove
my father worked. They called me fool,
set me down like a dunce on a wooden stool

While the hot dogs cooked, I fidgeted and frowned.
I knew one mistake didn't make me a clown. This rhyme must
die to let this damned poem fly home. But what with Audie's
warm eyes and my parents' dark sighs, I sat limp and alone in that sun
wondering what it was I had done
that so knocked the hell right
out of my fun

Guerneville, California

Words and Bees at the SF Marina

in the sun again
at the Marina we were
new and hot-glowing
in the mystery of potential
body to body we were still
standing hot when you said
there cold in the light
when you said that
my body wide open to you
feeling ready there
glowing with you
green round trees sweet
pressing the blue
we had made a place for ourselves
there to float when you said:
I was not finished, not complete.

Like a bee I'd been sapping seeping
honey coating sugar skin sublime
I needed you said more: my own
philosophy of life to live with.

My body humming double dahlias
My soul throbbed eloquent now to know
My brain writing a fertilized elegance

You said I needed something of a philosophy
to have about life later.
To know it. About it to know. A philosophy.

Those words stick the wind. Still.
Gray pawns in rich air.
Just when I was glowing
honey coating sugar skin.
Bee talk saturated busy. I be
actually wild in this mystery of potential.

Word talk fast-froze the wind
still, whip-lashed it to.

In the sun there that day at the Marina
when we were all new and hot
glowing out with ourselves.

When the Blue Light Went Off

> the uncertain meaning of yes. In a language spoken in words
> Frances Jaffer

Come full circle again
month by the clock
just in time to slide me in
and out of Italy again.

Slow train brought me here
and it rained and rained
and through the one slit eye
of my green old room
the blue light went off
out of the sky
and the buildings lay
in thin grey air
like a world of alley-cats
crying.

Who said it was
easy
before to me
to hang right into things?
to make blue from gray
with only desire to try on.

Come from a land
without winter
where cold doesn't seep in
so.
What do I know.

The lights fall
and wind
sweeps the ground
as months go round.

A slow trains coming
to take me back.

The sky sags meanwhile
like a puffy old man
dying.

Brindisi, Italy

Brought Up To Music

> I mean music that makes the mind
> continue in the move of melody.
> Francis Hosman

Brought up to music,
brought up to listen,
and to hear harder.

San Francisco walls hanging violins,
lush in brown wood and old time.
Brought up in sound and tone
a daily pitch to volume in melody.

Playing music, then, I was on a sound track,
on a straight line right into the moment
mainlining the present from the start.

Brought up to music,
touching the world into shape
through the tips of my polygraphic fingers.

Making It So Easy To See

> a kind of thinking, a mental complexion
> Willa Cather

upstairs in the study
two tall windows
whose blinds make it so easy to see
outside where the elms are busy
blowing fall around

on the green walls
black and white photos flat
echoes of family feeling gone
in all its unspoken eloquence.

and in San Francisco, there,
this consummate endlessness
what I think of sometimes
as the dark blue airs of eternity
shrouding the noisy silence of cities.
when you think of it when you do
it is a kind of singing without breathing
a blue note just out of focus.
light without sound.
It's like running up the sky with boots on
holding on to nothing with everything.
here and there it's life on the run.
the trick is to keep on running
with the clouds. the great bay boats
soft white cushions in the Pacific.

what I think of some times
when I forget the little girl who was me
sobbing without sound. in the silence
she has on a red hat. like autumn leaves,
blowing the light around on the run
holding on to nothing with everything.
she always did. what she could see about everything.

Birthday in Moscow

to Mother

there are times when what is poetry and love
comes only vaguely through the leaves,
through the maze
of yellow strident streets,
our old fatigue of trying
to make corners meet, fit
these windows of our lives close
firmly, but, I am here
in my speechful speechless way
with all the sentiments around
me and the easy road
of familiarity settles
on our travelling hearts
like some heavy sweet dust,
transplanted, through the swollen red
buds of your birthday flowers.

Homage to a Jamaican Stone-Carver

He sat near the docks,
whittling his world into shape,
building horses from a heap of white stone.
Hunched on his heels, working,
he rarely looked up
to see the crowds of tipsy pink
ladies glancing down.

I saw on a pier smoking grass,
my own silk dress pink,
damp in the sun.
I found him against a wall
flanked with ten little horses
and silver shaping tools.
We looked briefly at each other.
His hands moved down, sculpting.
Soon, I, too, disappeared
leaving dark hands firmly on the reins
to adjust the dimensions of his world.

For far more
            than
                that
                    hour
those white horses he made
imaged through my high fogs.
And, even now, when of my own making,
I neglect the blueness of the bare sky,
the light he carved into permanent shape
glistens in my sight.

Kingston

Sit-In: Sheraton Palace I: April 1964

I stretched out full length
on the sidewalk,
clutching my big woman's purse
and all I could see was the fog at first
and all I could feel was my girl friend's
thin wet hand pressing.
When the big men came,
the names men, in black leather coats.
Our two hundred eyes bore
upwards upon them.
The chief of police read penal
codes numbers who knows what
while we chattered like children
alone in the house
at home when the police come
whether we wanted to go,
to walk or not,
to balk or go slow.
The lawyer's eyes fell
out of his smug little face
like darts among us
as we rumored our way
to our judgment day
and great things moved
about us.

We were like an accident
there on the ground
with all the detectives
and curious hovering around.
We were abandoned as hostages
waiting to be claimed.
But the fires warmed us
and said you are right.
We took strength
and lay there in the night.

We were pregnant
with complete certainty,
and proud behind fear.

This one-time, one-sided
happiness took us all here.

When on a Long Night

When on a long night
Torn yellow grass

Far under the trees
There

Red peonies
Massing
Round and defiant

2012: Summer Without Rain

Sweet leaves, pale in your green.
In this summer without rain
Without the wet to cry by,
No well in which to sound the sigh

Chicken soup without dumplings
Bonnie on the road without Clyde
Perfect pitch without any volume
Of its own to set the tone by

The earth drizzles dry. A dunce's
Folly to trudge about six pence,
When it's ice cold here inside,
And my heart rains weeping crickets

Grand Rapids, Michigan

How Where We Were Was

> Love allows us to walk
> in the sweet music of our particular heart
> Jack Gilbert

On the street where you lived
we bought a house without the roots
you hated those false forever knots
and wanted to keep us stars in the trees
on the street where we lived
you made mulch and turned honey golden

and I surrounded us with flowers
and dried the herbs and seasonings of our summers
where we were, there, complete, in a love beyond the saying
as a music of smoky sounds, tenor sax bleeding
the whole tones of us making a love beyond words
to say for what I loved about your face. Holiday birds we thrived
in a green room. Half-moons rising in our eyes
sudden like solid smoke. On that street where we lived
together like stars in the trees. Such a singing without song-sound.

Two refugees planting each other fresh in the air.
A hoe-line could have not sown them any surer.
Strange star roots in the open. Once you said we
knew paradise. Just like that. A paradise. Star roots we were
surely, free to spread about with the honey and all those roses.

Grand Rapids

Green Fantasies: After Lewis Carroll

the precision of the forest
after leaves—it is crisp

the angle of those branches
curving into sight there
black tendrils bulging to
their size woven intricate into new

land-shape green fantasies
pitched on black fandangos—

swollen memories under Spanish
skies—eternal honeymoon
of talking stars and whimsical chaos

People

the tie between us is very fine, but a Hair never dissolves
Emily Dickinson

Death at 52

> to Mignonne

How are your bones doing down there?
Do the gophers come and warm your hollow cheeks
at night? Oh happy lady of the light,
I never dreamed your reckless strength
would fizzle, that I'd never laugh with you
again. You were a robust factory of delight.
Your long hands made colored tiles sing.
You fitted your love of this world
as clay takes solid form in the kiln.
You were activated, handsome and strong.
You gave your friends incentive.
Where have you gone?

You knew to brighten dark things.
You knew to turn yourself on.
You quivered at the source.
Oh woman, oh artist, oh godmother
by blood, what was it that took you,
Mignonne?

After the Heart Attack

Sometimes I drive myself crazy
imagining your blood, those silent red rivers.
Sometimes I'd like to go right through your skin
and know for sure that no jagged rocks
mar its even flow, that your channels
are wide and clear and clean, fit
for any worthy boat to sail away and go.
I would vacuum clean those veins for you.
I would build you dikes of polished stone.

But I can't come in. You're no toy doll
I can ever pull apart and know.
Your big heart beats behind awareness,
a thing no blood-test can ever show.
For we sleep with faith, wake to a mystery
again and again and then pull words from us
like clams from reluctant shells,
spooning cold litanies of sound into morning streets.
I fear that no two hearts can ever meet.

But I would see you beat
those gray gamblers at their actuarial games
to live on beyond them,
to move across dying
like sunspots slither over the sun,
I would hear you sing in the bathroom
and watch you go at night to walk alone
and wake to take you to me,
to press that impermeable skin to me,
to lie curled up in a prosperous silence
where we can rock and share and smell
where we can warble a few of our offbeat tunes
until the underground rivers run wild
and put a stop to our splendid show.

Conil de la Frontera

Uncle Sasha

Dear Sasha. Great Sasha.
You were something very special.
In Moscow's somber streets, flagellated
and smothered by summer's heat
and simmering peat bog fires,
you in that outrageously dignified hat
and cane, sickness pushing your bones,
overcame these pains and your daughter's
shame of you, to cut a swathe of finesse.

Haunted man who knew prison.
Proud man whose family split and fissured,
warred in the expected Russian Jewish way.
Sick man just three days out of bed.
I'd watch you as patriarch at your end
of all the tables heavy with food and talk.
You barely had the energy to smile sometimes
but you did and lectured about smoking
through all-conveying looks
of emotion when you caught our eyes.
My grandmother grew red from the efforts
of translation.
I babbled in smiles while the women
stroked and rubbed the top of my head.
I felt a volcano in you.
A bursting open in the long gray hair.

There.
Two worlds
barely touching in the air:
American blue jeans. Chekhov in English.
My Darling Clementine Slavicized on a dusty Victrola.
You'd look at me, the youngest,
wanting and getting something
but all my claims, living in Spain,
the bases, were wanting.

My mother's birthday dinner night
on the 25th floor of Moscow's swankest hotel
I read the speech you wrote
in English the whole afternoon long
and you stood up speaking in Russian,
saying things that made all the relatives cry,
the agility of Fred Astaire in your body's texture,
the weight of a visionary in your eye
and I felt an unexperienced pride in family,
the inherited forms.

Dead of pneumonia and gone
you fused so much and played so lonesome
light, so honor driven.
Man who knew pogroms and the family's
leaving you and war and jail and revolution.
Uncle who said my name like I used to
as a little girl, *Yinda, Yinda,*
I didn't get enough of you.

Echoes of Exotic

To Miriam Brim Chown

Igloo you. Echoes of Eskimo,
of the Asian exotic, cut
and curved cheekbones, boundless
beautiful. Your face feeling by far
too little for the rim of fire
shaking apart your silence
pushing

For My English Student

Mary Carmen, am I that strange
when I suggest balancing Samuel Beckett
on your head or when I ask you dead
serious what color the sky is
or to count the teeth in your head.
Sometimes your bright girl eyes
fade and flicker, saying more to me
than your wart-scarred hands twisting
the folds of your red plaid skirt.
Sometimes when I make you close
those eyes to hear the sounds come pure,
I think you think I'm crazy—
after all, after our first class
you told your mother my Spanish
wasn't like anybody you ever heard.

But you go on anyhow and count and conjugate
and name all the colors in the room.
I ask you how old is your brother
and if you like wine or fish or beer.
And you being 8 years old and free of boys,
yourself from your pony tail to your brown
worn boots, almost immaculate in your youth,
come, I think, to watch that funny foreigner
perform and clown, to see if you can match
the strangeness of my English sounds
and you know for an hour or two each week
I become the little girl and you the grownup
poised all proper and slightly skeptical
on the edge of your seat.

Cádiz

Part Payment

To Don

Who years later found me in the paper reading poetry at
I-Thou Coffee House and whom I visited in a VA hospital

Compact, with wire bones, you had the face
of a near criminal except for the sweet doe's
eyes that would sparkle and lust.
You loved motorcycles and speed and solitude.
A man of incomplete skills you were my
first lover in a dank drunken room
where I performed with such aplomb
you never knew it was a cherry
we so casually took together.
In the dark, I asked just what it meant
to have a "heart-on" and you laughed,
slapping my behind. Short-lived lovers,
when I had my fill, we drifted off
into others, without our moment of pain
or regret.

You grew enthusiasm as old ladies tend
their orchids: printing, Cuba, phony ID's
used to acquire tons of new TV sets to sell,
carrying big-time dope across the border
for small-time profits from other men.
These fruits were short-lived, too.
like brushing skin in the dark.
Somehow that doe's sense of honor in your eyes
kept you blinded to the way life juggles
fixed points and unambitious men.
Dead end street blues got you before the police
took both you and the haul
at some barren Texas border town.

Too clean to squeal on the commercial

zeals of your well-fed friends up north
one thing led to another as before—
handcuffs to a narrow cell in Leavenworth
and bells and bars and guards—
shared sunlight came about as often as Christmas
and the flowers of your hope withered
in unceasing and unfilled
promises of future parole.

You thoroughly marginal man,
to think our skins fit once
and I don't know how you signed your name
or how you approached your mornings.
How was it, then, to get deathly sick in the glands
alone, to be blasted with mustard gas
and to watch your own physique shrink,
lessen, until your joints weakened
and took you forever to bed, leaving
a gaunt man's face on a child's thin bones,
to walk into death at 32 in a military bed
where your listless legs dangled
without reaching the slippers on the floor
and your neck looked chicken-scrawny,
bony and grotesque?

Perhaps, hombre, it was your crowning
success, your way to elude all the many
buyers of your exceptional loneliness,
that terrible disintegration proving
you did, in fact, exist, but
you died, doe-eyed, as you lived, adrift
in the shadows, never really being
missed.

San Francisco

Don't Ask

Don't ask me to know your trees
or the green marbled statues of famous men.
Don't ask me to assume polite silence
before old gray churches or to join in your search
for the meaning of proud Dominic ruins
for in me you find a heretic from birth.
Born too soon set aside for life in an incubator
to watch the nurses fidget and grin
through tight lipped walls of glass,
I required special air from the start.

Not for me the immediate succor
of a mother's swollen breast.
I slid loyally into years of asthma
and staying at home. Instead
of school's compulsions and off-witty games
I patted chickens to death
in an excess of love and counted
the squares on the ceilings over my head.
I feasted on solitude all youth long.
Solitude and the friendship of rock and roll songs.
Even when I tried later to join the ranks
somehow it all went wrong.

So when you ask me to tell you more
of my days, I'm all out of practice
in these ways. I've kissed too much
solitude with my premature teeth..
Just a rough peasant at your feasts,
at your ceremonious guests
I'm without the proper answer
to your slightest requests.
So don't ask me, go on to seek
the meaning of your own life song.
Ring those ancient church bells
with the light of your mind

and play your particular music
on those mysterious walls of stone.

And let me go on bullshitting
myself out of business
with my own fantastic, self-
comforting sounds.

On the Other Side of Language

> I speak only one language, and that is not my own
> Jacques Derrida

for Barbara

That way too white tree
was not a natural thing. It was
sure to be a penance, a pear, too much of itself,
like some kind of permanent stand out.
A piece of sharp metal grating
on a dark hill sparse with weeds,
which were pale to a curious
buckskin-man who fingered them
as he felt. Among the bare weeds. Discontent.
Somehow he had learned that disgust for outcasts.
A contempt for cripples. For all those who do not fit.
all the unmatched, born-to-be-groping-souls
like we all are, stranded on the other side of language,
bleached in the daily clumsiness of trying to say our own.
To find a way to speak sure.
To fasten the sun once and for all.

So that unsymbolic white tree
in the silence without branching to bear any leaves or shade
reminded him of a childless woman drying in hard light.
Hard to bear her white aging.
Hard to detoxify such solitude
peaking in the sun without taking off,
to him she was like a bird spinning inchoate,
trapped as she seemed to him to be
in such naked speech without saying,
words without sounds, all-day-long Latin monologues
swirled, speaking themselves silent, he thought.

But she burrowed and drew her language in from
the blue sky she slept in and came out to plant and sow

what she had to say for herself in the clear darkness
of muses and mystery. In her whitest way, she raged over the edges of
what she was to be. Of all that could be said to say. In her quiet white,
she burned a hole in the dark to go
beyond men and women, words and children and
time, and whatever is lonely, to well herself up accidentally in the air,
a free-to-be white beyond owners and words and withering,
white in the ways of dreamers and whales and misfits,
white to hold on and white to let be. White to burn a saying,
white as a language she could sleep with as her own, lucid in the fog.

Grand Rapids

The Young Widow

The Spanish telephone operator
has got an ache in her
husband's death at 34
infarction coming on
the Sunday it never should
strike such a low took him off
and black cloth bears her
afterwards hole the opens
grief falls through, spattering
the wake of the words heard
with alone the telephone
three young kids mouthing
how dry I am
and the Spanish telephone operator
grits herself her pieces
ringaling ding a dong

Salamanca

The Little Lamb

After the blacksmith left the air thick with tar,
Blackie kicked his new–shod hoofs in the dirt,
sprinting the length of the corral.
Grandfather heard me cough.
Horse liniment would fix me up fast, he said,
chuckling as I went into bed.
I've counted 56 holes in the tiles overhead so far.
Mother, can you come here for a minute, please?
I've eaten three pieces of bread in bed.
She bustles in the kitchen,
high heels clicking on the linoleum floor.
Two glasses of fruit juice, a back rub
and a game of cards so far.
I've got a pile of books and a pair
of lungs to call with.
Mother, I want….
Hushed: voices in the kitchen excite me
and make my sex warm.
The room grows stale and hot.
I lie very still and hear the crickets
imagine the garden snakes sliding
through the tall grasses in the yard.
Lie very still and watch the stars grow
out there in the sky.

Maybe tomorrow I'll go to school again….
walk down the dirt pathway to the old bridge
and across the stream to the high wire fence
and into the gray yard where girls hang
from their knees on the jungle gym
singing little chants before the bell rings.
And sit in the back of the class
near the open windows
where the sun streams in

A voice from up front asks

"where you been all this time"
and the room rocks with laugher.
I tuck my unused notebook under the chair
and a piece of hair falls over my eyes.
My feet sweat in the knee high socks
mother insists I wear.
Two girls in front
whisper loudly and pass notes
around the room.
The boys I climb the big oak tree
with at home won't even talk to me here.
My mouth tightens
and I start playing with my hair.
The room buzzes.
I close my eyes and grandfather
brushes up the horses, waxes saddles.
I close my eyes and the dog barks
behind the house.
I close my eyes…
Trees scrape the window.

Lights are out now in the kitchen.
I hear my parents in bed,
Mother saying *Paul, no, she can't go.*
She still coughs bad in the morning.
Her voice creeps under the door.
I hear her like a whisper.
Silence fills this room,
fills the house.
The fluorescent lamb
framed on the wall
shines on me,
mouth forever fixed
just above the flowers

Strange Man

You've been waited on too long
wont even do breakfast on your own
wont answer the doorbell
when I'm with a poem.
So what is this warring of yours
around the house
this weekly round of complaining
about?

You want the fire hot
before the coals get hot
If it's not the noise I make
then it's the time I take.

Oh poem hanging half-way
tell the strange man
with stranger ways
that beans come with slow cooking
that his whims are wearing
the time away.

Conil de la Frontera

To the Second Doorman

I know how it feels
caretending, like a woman
a boyman, how the desire comes
to pinch pockets for stray coins,
how you've got to greet them
cordially and listen too hard,
how you protect a corner
for yourself, collecting gee-gaws
to fill it in,
how you rummage through the laundry,
how you make schedules and wait
glower and feel unreasonable proud.

I bet you'd like to see
the elevators jam, the phone lines break.
I bet you'd like to take
our combed-over garbage
and shove it.

You turn into a rat.
An inhabitor of dark furtive
places.
You dally.
You diddle.
You grow imperceptibly
into hate.

Abortion

Those eggs you threw at the wall
were hurled for me and the broken door
where your fist rammed in like horns
was for me and your face blank with anger
was my seedy offspring too.

And just a moment before the morning
was fresh as though rain had cleaned us
all last night.

Incredulous. I say *cut, stop,*
but we've already passed out of ourselves,
passed away into he's and she's.
The lines are all drawn clearly now.

The eggs stick to the walls like fetuses.
We've miscarried today.
Your back is a fortress.
I've got nothing to say.

Cádiz

School Days

When I was
young and sick,
asthmatic and whooping in bed,
night after morning,
week after week,
I read at least one
book every everlasting day
and in every damned position
I could invent for myself,
read Heidi, Little Women,
the Nancy Drew stories and Babar,
always just
too sick to wash my hair
and the dandruff caked up
for me to pick
until even my face got greasy
and by night I was sticky
and bleary eyed all over.
I'd fall asleep
and dream
of being the best
dressed girl
in the whole fifth grade
and wake up in a sweat
to believe
I might never make it
out the front door
to take the chance of winning.

El Cerrito

Standing Out in the Straight

Haunts of people intense in spring light,
Straw fields and thatched roofs,
Wood fences standing at a slant.
The strangeness of people surge.
Your pale hat whiter than the hills and the sand.
The white of uniqueness. An unsullied tone,
Like you were, holding on to my red shirt
Your body planted firm in my mind—
Woody Herman swinging with Django Reinhardt.
Soulful on syncopated. In that strange balance
we made, standing out in the straight.

Conil de la Frontera

Missing

I

How long it was, that night.
The birds on the block
cackling and hooing till daylight,
fire trucks screaming in the city,
whining and whistling through
every corner of the bed
I tried to rest in.
And Herman, the huge crazy black Afghan
next door, looney too
He heard the wild sounds,
bayed madly at the moon
in his highest dog croon
while I dipped against the bed,
choking out sleep,
listening to the whoosh of cars in the street.

Are you dead, I said.
Did you fall off a cliff
and land on a beach
somewhere on a walk you took?
Did you take off with someone
or did you just take off?

My knees tighten together.
I am shaking, smoking.
I am in the middle of night.
Where are you?

II.

Running downstairs calling you.
6 AM. I fall off a cliff,
landing alone at the bottom
of the stairs in a morning light
pale blue and moist,

the color and taste of dawn.
The light is too gentle
for this violent surprise.
Alone in my time now?

I really don't know.
Don't know what to do with myself
now. My time is passing. Fast.
The daylight's coming,
exposing every hard surface in the house.
Every thing in place.
Herman sleeping on the lawn.
A perfect quiet morning.
No evidence you are not here.

I must be in hell,
I am hell.
The world has stopped for me.

My terrible waiting.

III.

When I got the policeman on the phone
he said how long has he been missing
how long been missing
he said
we'll issue a routine search
what is your name he said
these things
so formally.
I said don't think
I will do that now.

IV.

You are the only
person in the world

I could tell
you are dead to.

V.

I take a window seat
on the bus going downtown
to meet you.
Here and there.
People amble in the heat.
The broken leather seat I lean on.
Attention. At ease.
Attention. At ease.
The wind begins to blow
from light to light
down Market Street.

Your gray tweed jacket
brushes me, scratching
stab of memory
There is one of you and one of me.
One of me and one of you.
Together still makes two.

VI.

You stayed in a hotel
to be away from me,
to be, for I was missing.
Sitting together
in the Chinese restaurant
all the questions
I would have asked you
are for me.

We eat lightly.
I have not been
the keeper of my cabin.

My terrible waiting.

My mind turns on itself.
A bowl of soup,
an old scratch of a poem.
Your gray jacket
brushing on my hair.

The wind rustles the papers in the street,
inevitable, bitter-sweet,
my love,
growing.

San Francisco

Meeting

I.
Almost out the door, I saw you
headed for the other wing of the building.
We were only one courtyard apart.
I had not seen you for months,
could have left safely,
pretended you were not around.
I watched you move, forward,
surely in a new blue suit,
dark glasses over your eyes.
My mind churned.
If I went now, no one would know.
But you are getting older.
Suddenly I ran across the courtyard.
Holding on tight to my books and purse,
I ran to meet you.

II.
Daddy, I try to tell you
and I fail.
I try to tell you
guts are personal.
They don't always show.
I tell you I'm different now,
and you wanting to know what that means
say, *well, how to do you feel about life?*
Then I can't begin to tell you anything.
I don't want to know anymore.

Daddy, I'm not a political radical
and you're disappointed.
I even made a joke of being Camus' stranger
but it wasn't funny.
Neither of us laughed.
You asked me where my passion went.
How can I tell you that?

        Daddy, I've talked myself out
all my life
with words.

        I'm engaged to a new silence.
The rules are simple.
Say just what you believe,
don't say just anything.
Believe me.
I'm not saying I'm holy.
I'm still afraid of my voice.
But hear me. Hear me now.
Daddy, hear my voice.

You lean across the bench in the courtyard
and give me a fast kiss on the cheek.
I watch you move away,
your briefcase heavy with books,
you on your way to work
and I on my way to it,
I watch you go away,
your steps slower this time.
What more can we say, now, Daddy.

III.
On the bus going home
I listen for myself,
checking to see
how truthful I am,
checking to see
how I am.

San Francisco

Roots Taking Hold

to Heather on her 80th birthday

All at once, Heather, and I think
Of green moss, the sweetness
Of all that green gathering.
The sureness of roots and tendrils
Touching in the gullies
Where it all begins.

I think of this gathering,
The roots and shoots there,
That quiet itching in the soil,
In this green moss and I remember Heather
Spreading her gift, bringing us together.

And I think of roots taking hold surely,
Spreading in the green moss.

Grand Rapids

Wood Sight

> Is there a happiness
> later on that is neither fierce nor reasonable
> Jack Gilbert

I.
When you went gone bye
I bought you wood:
Hairless paupers squirmed in the sun;
A gray mare hoof-huffed, pawing at the dust;
One alabaster finch frozen in night fright
rocks speechless in mid-flight.
A mint shadow of the moon awakens
and spreads a shell husk-sliver green—

The sky burst open and rivers pitch-black
jostle, bleeding vertical and ragged in the skyline-
Pandemonium spreading across the foreparts-
A tumult of silent sparrows floats
upwards, wings opening into a tempest—
mysterious impulse poised on blind morning brick.
Patchy pieces of green pinplode in the air,
sharp like seasonal sparkles, drifting dim downward.
All the lead gaskets ever soldered gyre-wipe
shapeless pockets of acrid air into a light
far too saturated now to see.

II
Once, roasted smug, blind in sunlit oblivion
I would have built a kind of trap
to keep you, I would have, a shiny locket
of a thing, safe, secluded, shelter-away sham,
The shrill shame of it, hard, smooth, impervious, prison rig,
away from those quixotic currents fluid and fluent.

After the time when you went gone bye
after the shadow of the moon awoke
the hairless paupers who squinted

acrid into the burning morning
And I bought you wood--
not just any old wood to hold you,
I wanted to meet you head-on in the deep,
to build something infinitely far beyond sturdy—
something to grow into, to endure
beyond before because.

III

That baroque morning, I bought you wood,
touched the porous resinous cellular
graininess of it, the gnarls and knots, bulbs and sweet chips,
perspicuous patinas and flaunting figures,
the very sap of it grows soft, dusty and natural in the seeing.
Touching two matching side-tables,
one by each in sheer tactile deference,
their drawers sliding open cobbled, unique.
I grew there like a sapling rooted at long last,
rooted and bound free in my origins.
Slathered in such diffusion of wood sight,
suffusion of sycamore and rosewood
curly cherry and ash-cottage oak—

The world begins simply to spin, slow, long, textured,
grainy and porous in my eyes touching.
On a morning of hairless paupers and alabaster
finches rocking speechless in mid-flight
I went out a closed door, past gray walls and steel-magenta dikes
and bought you all the wood I could fit
in a fast flipper-flopper of a heartbeat
and fastened it all free in its origins:
braided, branded, burned in this solemn wood vision,
sweet lullaby of stillness, apocalyptic morning bright,
all the way open metaphysical treat,
being here now for all the now there is.

Cherished alchemy just come upon
the morning you went gone bye

and I bought you wood all grainy and porous
to be here for now where the world begins to spin
and shiver sweetly in its consonance,
soft in wood-inflected light

Grand Rapids

Knowings

When a thought hears itself see
Susan Howe

Out West When Clouds Rolled Over

Once she had a seamless mind:
Clouds rolled into her thinking
like opposites attracting. And hitching.
There was that openness of all beginnings.
And those crisp little white cockle shells. And then
that low fog. It was spreading around
like when once you could touch time without rules or referees,
like when you used to dance alone with your eyes closed
serenading crazy in your room late, the doors shut, the music on fire,
and you moved around in there, bumping the walls
like salmon swarming and flapping up the ladder.

Just that. Somehow just
to be seamless that way. Fiercely in the free.

Clouding in open fog.

Grand Rapids

Some Times Writing

> Lay these words down so that they will be less cloud-like.
> Beverly Dahlen

Sometimes writing in the rain
I hear the quiet people
Whispering dream
Memories.

Red husks of memory.
A violence of fragments.

All that they wanted.
All that mattered.
Dream timing in a sequence—
Echoes and silhouette and heartbreak.
As one sometimes,
As we, are, sometimes,
Writing in the rain.

Grand Rapids

Sometimes We Can't Keep Up

sometimes the important just can't
be said even when it's so
big or just because it floods
watery over the sheer names of things,
while the great stuff, that which
makes the homeless burn soot-filled fires
every night on dark scarred streets,
what makes the old dreams
turn into sleep-defying drama,
what makes us know ourselves
exactly as we hope ourselves to be,

sometimes we just can't keep up,
even when it's so big we sink
into a hard swoon of regularity and
that important stuff, what we wake to
applauding loud in the light of morning
in a winter bed after finishing
the job of our dreams,
hovers like a stranger, as a
particularly solitary child looks,
over-sensing the present and
pondering it all voiceless

Grand Rapids

To Say Thinking

> a thought is the bride of what thinking
> Beverly Dahlen

It was at first as though no one.
It was as though there was no hearing
at the table where no one listened.
It was as though her sound
was too quiet.
All her speaking tactile in that bed
shining like that white lamb on the wall.
All the talking behind the sky moments.
To have a say beyond the clutter of talk.
Far behind the anonymous stars in their spin she reached.
She had to learn all without teaching
something of her own,
a language to say it in. A wild mind
where everything mattered: stars and lambs and silhouettes.
She was by herself in that thin bed wheezing
and taking it all in, "deep," Wyman said you were.
Deep. Maybe one of those grown-in-the-wild miracles
in a jungle fluent in her own making.

Ever since she found the words to speak public,
they rolled out of her faster than
she could ever say them to know.
Her voice seemed to sound a ways,
low like crickets in a run of drifting.

Grand Rapids

Where We Are In

when it was the beginning of forever
and I forgot all about the morning
when I woke up to the sounds of
street grinders crying out loud in shady
Granada and the butane trucks blared
about *amor* and *corazón* and banging
and wanting in this floating light
lit with some longing while
the morning merges into itself
and a woman sings of a love
that always is. over and again.
of a love that always is.
she sings strong, and clear.
here, always where we are, in
the beginnings of forever.

Grand Rapids

Writing To

> I tie knots in the strings of my spirit
> to remember
> Jack Gilbert

Write to. Write about not.
It just begins. And she does.
Little all in her combat.
Not about. But to.
Her troubled eyes.
Close to get. Come to see
The fire raging.

In a brood she was
Turned outside to stay in,
Playing with her suspenders
In Cousin Belle's house in the city,
Violins pressed to the walls and Gonnie
Staunch there, braiding her exploding hair.

Only the lonely, little in bay windows,
With special keys of solitude,
Tell stories with their fingers,
Plucking passions in the sunset.

Grand Rapids

On Reading Old Poems

Surprised by all those words,
the barren complications, by the way
I tried too hard to make things more,
yes, say it out, to be creative,
I must have been living indoors too long,
my eyes peering through tree leaves,
my nose breathing old book dust,
tongue lacquered with liquidy discretions
so that these poems seem mummies
in a glass cage, all wrapped and wound,
yellowing at the seams, too suspect of fraud
to be the fertile that poems need be, to be.

I would have them leaves, transparent
in the light. I would grow them green
to catch the sight. Their sound ring
like colored bead doors swaying in a village
wind at night. I would let them go like children
or bubbles in the air, convinced of their shape,
if I knew they really came from feeling,
where animals quake. We'd join
and climb, threading words on the sky
and disperse like summer fireworks,
bright and spent in an unrepeatable fall,
hailing down a small touch of glory,
giving our all.

Conil de la Frontera

Shore-Lines in the Sand

> One day it will cease to feel like a language;
> it will become the way things are
> J. M. Coetzee

Why would I want to write about flat fields
And bright color, to suggest limits and consequence
Why would I want to make pictures
As though I were an artist copying the wind
As though things could be anything
As though there could be shore lines in the sand

As though Camus could ever live without light
As though Cezanne would not paint his canvas thicker and thicker
As though birds lead photographable lives on their perches
Bobbing up on demand to entertain white-faced children
When, backstage, birds beak their worlds bloody
Batter and rush the air in hypnotic trance.

Life is no transparent stillness
with the hollow grace of imaginary holiday.
The forces of flat tussle with the agitations of circumstance.

I want my poems to touch that surge,
that place where blood first moves into sleep,
where heart spears memory as it gropes into time.
I want the crash of titans, life in the round,
to be in the brunt of it,
inside the thunder before the storms,
I want to sustain the bang in the beginning.
Hot headed and sure fired,
poems spin far from flat fields,
to hover inside time and knowing
with the blinding precision of dreams.

Writing in Place

> Mostly I love how
> we burst the prisons of our skins and shine.
> Kathy Fagan

It's about weighing things,
It's about equals,
like to like, peach to peach,
swimming out loud in the ocean
and floating even in the tides

It's about writing in place
like fitting right into your skin, heart speech in morning sleep,
writing word for word on the air.

It's like exactly.
Blue cats in the clouds.
It's like nothing extra
the orange white under the rind there,
that long-clean sweet and fresh,
or Samuel Beckett unwording
the world playing his flute magical.

It's about holding some rhythm
in a groove, sharps folding into flat
at last Etta James and life is all in the song
like Leslie Howard dancing his elegant face
and Humphrey Bogart gliding through his silhouettes.

It's about writing in place,
here where here is,
this balance, ripe sweet corn cobbing,
wild geese gandering
This sheer sun light
when somehow
you can be as never before

standing out still with yourself
writing in your place
beyond all the words and kissing the sky.

Grand Rapids

When The Sun Is

> Maybe there is no sublime; only the shining of the amnion's
> tatters.
> Galway Kinnell

When the sun is bright
and the sky blue
as the deepest dreams of water
can make it
believe is a poem
whole in itself.

When colors dim
think poetry is
what you do
with the blackness
before and after
things occur.

For poems
take hold
in sound and light
of the patterns the world
makes
as we pass through,
like stones across water.

Poems
let people
and places
and reflections live
as lived in—
taken hold of—
like footprints in sand
or the wash, hung, there,
on the line,
piece by piece

shape against shape,
cutting wedges into blue sky.

Poems
remind me and you
something was and is
we are,
here,
in the sunlight,
in this vanishing air.

El Cerrito

There Was Never Enough Home

in the shadow
a motor obliterate
the sound of growing
there was never enough
home to come back to
when you could be you
with them inside at a table
to breathe in breathing
something like stones
what we come to be
like without thinking
she was lucky to have lived out
alone in her silence

Grand Rapids

And There They Were

> Let's see the very thing and nothing else.
> Let's see it with the hottest fire of sight.
> Wallace Stevens,

presented with the physical, with the body of things
hot in August specifically those moo cows

udders hanging fat and swollen purple,
heavy with Christ recumbent, *agonizante*

even with this drone of pain like a toll
no one could ever keep up—

Michael row the boat ashore hallelujah
here in the din, this heave and throb
of trouble, terrible pulses pitch about turgid.

To have become an extra in my life
without the sleeping dogs to let lie

down down in the bleach of it. The die deads
and the feed fed a tangle of temporary temper
meant to turn about terrible in the twitch

I am pain which takes the gears over whole-
hog wild and I am the child I once was

stuck again to fetch seeing on my own,
staring blind through the physical,
rapt in a pool of danger;

Ocarinas and concertinas may yet rescue
with their after-voices set to mouth me
so that my brain before I come to know

anything to think about to say, that

there is this completeness, this beauty
beyond the eerie tumescence of those moo ones.
Hallelujah amen *hosannah* for these voices ever

after sounding that prayer I have always wanted
to ask for more of, as in an exaltation row row the boat
and wait here, psalms for to listen, canticle as to lullaby to
bait this whippled heart to crackle
and play August chords loud

crescendo into these credences of
a summer light
voracious enough to hear like the sound of this sun
landing before your eyes saucer-smooth,
cucumber cool on a searing white moon.

Grand Rapids

Flower Juice

> Everything was without shadow
> Virginia Woolf

send a rose to the jack of all trades
he will know it for a flower
and wear its perfume in his shoe

stepping on the scent
the rose still breathes
the jack trades

a few thin petals
turn a little flower juice

San Francisco

Politics is What People Do

> and I know how much
> I envy
> those for whom politics
> is everything
> and those
> for whom it is nothing
> Mark Linenthal

Walking on the sands of Stinson Beach
the wind mounted invisibly.
We had risen from sand beds and blankets
to catch our toes in the soil
to see the Pacific stretch
and reach out exactly to the horizon
like geometry.

You turned to me
and I to you
and one of us said
looking out into the distance
what if all of a sudden
the enemy should come
in an enormous white boat
plant a flag in the sand
and capture the whole United States
in a minute

And what if
faster than our eyes move
their flags were pitched
from sea to sea
and we knew it.
Then there would be simply
two things left to do:
be captured mute
like the rest

or climb aboard
and start things anew.

I looked to you
and you to me.
sure enough
we knew what we'd do
walk down to where the water starts,
arms high above our heads
yelling out we'll come with you
in every language
we ever knew
until they took us aboard
or the sun turned blue.

Bodega Bay

To Be or To Be

It is impossible
to be all
that we would like
to be, dream
to be

It is in our reach
to take hope off
its soft sad pedestal

and in the grind of our minds
wrench ourselves back
into this one chance
always present

San Francisco

Too Many Moons

> for Jack Gilbert who went further

Too many moons in his poems, he said they said.
Too much sky. But what if he had lived on islands
under the sun with fishermen. What if he had heard
silence sounding in the water. What if there were no words.
What if to him a southern moon stared
At infinity in that night light
And held the chaos of lovers.

Grand Rapids

About the Lion

They say our hearts are golden
They say we roar
They say we eat all our soup
with relish.
They say we have the gift
of gravitating.
Today, however, my heart is poor.
Every bone bleeds.
The back of my spine
broken,
the calf muscles sore.
If I can never take soft
bites
of the chunk of this
rotten
life
that picks our hopes up
like featherweight clouds
in a spring storm
that makes us dare to reach
to dream haunted
fantasies of more
I would take that metaphorically
mangy tail and wind my bulging
heart up in it
to keep it warm and right and tight.
I would.
I would.

Seattle

And He Thought He Said

The feathers don't scratch
he said, twice. He said, he added, he
thought the room was on
fire and all mighty feathers,
they fester. Again he. And so.
He said like that the fur was flying.
And how could they fight beyond
them selves. Their ken-kin. On the side
could they, he thought of doctors,
of loss, in the morning before coffee
and bandits there. And of the ships that don't
go bump in the night. All those things that don't
continue. He wondered wandered even.
When he thought of the end of lullabies.
What the babies did with their tongues in the silence.
Where are the words he didn't trouble to think to say,
Those things that don't continue after moonlight
get swallowed in the beginning. A lurch
of apparently luminous sidekicks they dance
without music with the scurry of crickets.

Grand Rapids

A Kind
of a Love Poem

purple cloth
and yellow daisies
fly in the edge of my eye

dilly dilly
willy nilly
my eye starts
in the endless color

but lavender blue
golden flower
what can I
say to you?

San Francisco

To an Unknown Painter

In the picture the two monks pose
against sharp grey cliffs,
their white robes full as Renoir women.
The gentle spread of linen
almost avoids the pain contained
in the wounds sustained
where a knife blade cleaves
into one monk's head,
sticking snug as an ax in wood
and where the arrow plunged
in the other's heart
stringing his guts
into beads of pain.

Still the two men pose
bucolic in that painter's eye
with a trace of joy flush
in their cheeks

There must have been a light for him
To leave those spoiled old monks
so bloodless
or he knew already
how the end would come
and left their blood alone
and all the rituals of pain
to keep a light for centuries
on those pale and willing men.

Granada

The Gift

I'm full to burst.
The image is old.
Even I can see
purple grapes hanging
water-mottled in the picnic grove.
Good for the eating they are
it is said. But what of this hungry
stretching inside, as though I myself
were pregnant of me
kicking you and you me
on this narrow balcony
waiting for a poem

My world has grown you
veins and seeds and nodes of your own.
Your freedom is under my skin's
limits. I touch the black rail
with a brown hand,
and you come up behind me
and those grapes in summer
join you
and me through the skin
and rail and metaphor
in yet another skin's grin,
a poem.

Conil de la Frontera

Red Around the Center

> To Henri Matisse.
> Dessert Harmony in Red

Red around the center
where the woman sits there,
lumbering in her frame.

She stares as an object might
back to the bone in a hard time.
She is in the red way off center
Out of line in her own painting.

So odd, so indelibly strange.
Red, red a gentleman said
And from somewhere Alice remembered
"You are old, Father William."

And, so, she shudders red in her place
staring now at something new.
In the twilight a call of birds,
not Wallace Stevens' "pigeons sinking
downward to darkness on extended wings."

But a sudden outcry of faith upwards, as of loons
pitched long together in a wildness wandering,
a memory of music pure in the fog

And of their touching everything everywhere,
their bulky physical pressing into each other.
And of their faces, gone wide-eyed in a wonder.

Grand Rapids

Out of the Wind

Train the mind
To patterns not pieces,
To catch the shape of things,
The lines that run among,
A common spring.

A camel's angle clarifies
The lion's massive curve.
The cloud's face depends
On the blue light behind.

We see and later may say
When the leaves have gone
What those faded yellow skins
Align.

In the leaves
Spreads a sudden movement
Of the mind.

San Francisco

How To Say What

To say nothing the same.
In the space. To repeat nothing And everything.
Put it there over the moon with the heart outside.
When you. And it's all read/red. Granny Smith is gone.
Took a kind of a powder. If I only were in a dark
of my own making. Making out fireflies touch things sticky.
Do tell how to say what: do Prague lights shine spatial
hollows in Slavic moonlight when nothing says
anything anymore. More than more. Two is not one again.
Grasshoppers have thin legs and I want to go home. For Christmas
in a dark of my own. Making without silent night. To say nothing
the same. When you. If I were only in a dark of my own. Making.

Grand Rapids